LEON

Soups, Salads & Snacks

NATURALLY FAST RECIPES

LEON

Soups, Salads & Snacks

NATURALLY FAST RECIPES

By Henry Dimbleby, Kay Plunkett-Hogge, Claire Ptak & John Vincent

PHOTOGRAPHY BY GEORGIA GLYNN SMITH · DESIGN BY ANITA MANGAN

conran
OCTOPUS

Contents

Introduction

Leon was founded on the belief that food should taste good and do you good. We wanted to make it easy for everyone to eat this way.

The recipes in this book are designed to help you do just that. They are created from a small number of easy-to-find ingredients and the vast majority have five steps or fewer. It is food that you can make quickly from scratch. None of the recipes take more than 20 minutes to prepare – with the exception of Benny's Scotch Eggs (see page 44) and Ana's Cheese Empanadas (see page 46), which reward the investment handsomely. You can let your oven do the rest and kick back with a glass of wine or some fiendish mental puzzle – depending on preference.

It is also a little book. We want it to become a companion. One that you take with you on holiday, or for the weekend. Or, painful though it is to consider, to give to that beloved child on the day they fly the nest.

While quick, the recipes (selected from the best in the full-sized Leon cookbooks) have been chosen for their variety. The soups range from the scented and exotic: Apple's Persian Onion Soup (see page 10), to the homely and comforting: Bacon & Root Veg Soup (see page 23).

In the salad chapter you will find things that are absurdly quick and perfect for a TV supper; try Bean Salad with Pickled Onions (see page 26) or Mackerel Skies Salad (see page 39). For something more glamorous that could form the centre of a summer lunch try Laura's Jewelled Salad (see page 28).

In the snacks chapter we hope to provide a little inspiration for those in-between moments of unfocused peckishness. You will find imaginative toppers for spuds (see page 48) and toast (see page 54). There are quick dips (see page 56) and the Leon best-seller Fish Finger Wrap (see page 52).

Whichever recipes take your fancy, we hope you use this book again and again. And that in 20 years' time it is still in your kitchen – dog-eared and sauce-splattered, but loved. Happy cooking.

Henry & John

SOUPS

Apple's Persian Onion Soup

SERVES 4 AS A STARTER • PREPARATION TIME: 10 MINUTES • COOKING TIME: 40 MINUTES • ♥ ✓ WF DF GF

A favourite recipe from the restaurants – very healthy, and great if you are feeling under par.

4 large **onions**
2 tablespoons **olive oil**
1 heaped teaspoon **turmeric**
1 heaped teaspoon **ground fenugreek**
1 teaspoon **dried mint**
1 litre **chicken or vegetable stock**
1 **cinnamon stick**
½ a **lemon**
sea salt and **freshly ground black pepper**

1. Peel the onions and slice thinly. Put the onions into a large pan with the olive oil. Add some salt and pepper, cover the pan and cook gently for at least 15 minutes, stirring occasionally.

2. Add the turmeric, fenugreek and mint, and cook for another few minutes without the lid.

3. Add the stock and cinnamon stick, bring to the boil, then reduce the heat and simmer for at least 20 minutes.

4. Add the juice of half a lemon and season with salt and pepper and serve. We like to leave the cinnamon stick in.

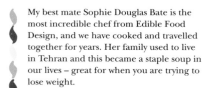

My best mate Sophie Douglas Bate is the most incredible chef from Edible Food Design, and we have cooked and travelled together for years. Her family used to live in Tehran and this became a staple soup in our lives – great for when you are trying to lose weight.

APPLE

TIPS

* Add some chopped fresh mint and parsley at the end to liven things up.

* Apple adds a teaspoon of sugar for added sweetness – we leave this out.

Kay's Minestrone Maltese

SERVES 4 • PREPARATION TIME: 20 MINUTES • COOKING TIME: 30 MINUTES

When Kay's parents first moved to Gozo in Malta, they made friends with some of the local farmers who had fields on the slopes below the house. One of those farmers taught them the basis of this soup. It's not a thin soup; its hearty, filling and packed with flavour.

1–2 tablespoons **olive oil**
1 **onion**, finely chopped
1 **carrot**, finely chopped
1 stick of **celery**, finely chopped
2 cloves of **garlic**, finely chopped
1 teaspoon **fresh rosemary**, finely chopped
1.2 litres **vegetable stock**
1 x 400g **tin of tomatoes**
1 **bay leaf**
1 piece of **Parmesan rind** (optional)

1 x 400g tin of **cannellini beans**, drained and rinsed
80g little **pasta shapes**
150g **peas**
1 **courgette**, cut into chunks
a good grating of **nutmeg**
70g **bacon lardons** (optional)
a few **celery leaves**, chopped
freshly grated **Parmesan cheese**, to garnish
salt and **freshly ground black pepper**

1. Heat the oil in a large, heavy-based pan over a low to medium heat. Add the onion, carrot, celery and garlic and soften gently for about 5 minutes. Then add the rosemary and cook for another 2 minutes or so to release its oils.

2. Now add the stock, tomatoes, bay leaf and the Parmesan rind (if you're using it), and cook for about 5 minutes. Season with salt and pepper, add the beans, and simmer for another 15 minutes or so.

3. Add the pasta, and cook, as per the instructions on the packet, until done. About 5 minutes before the end, add the remaining vegetables.

4. Finally, add a couple of gratings of fresh nutmeg and stir it into the soup, and then season to taste.

5. Serve garnished with chopped celery leaves and a grating of Parmesan.

TIPS

* Minestrone simply means 'a big soup', so you can pretty much put into it anything you like. Instead of the peas, why not add about 400g of trimmed and sliced kale or chard?

* If you want to add some lardons, cook them in a separate pan and add them as a garnish. This means you can serve this as a completely vegetarian soup.

Marion's Lentil Soup

SERVES 6 • PREPARATION TIME: 10 MINUTES • COOKING TIME: 1 HOUR • ✓ WF GF

If chicken noodle soup is Jewish penicillin, this is North London Protestant penicillin. Marion, John's mum, makes this for the family when it's cold, or when people have colds. Make lots in advance, and get it out of the freezer whenever the feeling or the need arises.

1 tablespoon **olive oil**
1 large **onion**, chopped
2 **leeks**, sliced
1 clove of **garlic**, crushed
4 rashers of **smoked streaky bacon**, chopped
2 **carrots**, sliced
3 sticks of **celery**, sliced
225g **red lentils**, washed and drained
½ teaspoon **grated nutmeg** or **turmeric**
1.25 litres **vegetable** or **chicken stock**
salt and **freshly ground black pepper**

1. Gently heat the oil in a large heavy-based pan. Add the onions and leeks and let them cook gently until they're transparent. Add the garlic and bacon and cook on a medium heat for another 3–4 minutes.

2. Now stir in the carrots and celery, and cook for a further 2–3 minutes. Finally, stir in the lentils, and add the nutmeg or turmeric.

3. Pour in the stock and bring the soup to the boil. Simmer with the lid on for about 30–40 minutes, or until the lentils and vegetables are tender. Season the soup with salt and pepper, then blend until smooth.

TIPS

* Marion prefers to use an immersion blender for this recipe. If you're using a stand-alone blender be very careful not to over-fill it so you don't spatter the kitchen (and yourself) with boiling soup.

* For a thicker consistency use more carrots and/or celery.

Leek & Potato Soup

SERVES 4 • PREPARATION TIME: 20 MINUTES • COOKING TIME: 45 MINUTES • WF GF V

This is the simplest and most soothing soup we know – perfect for a stormy winter's day.

1 **leek**, about 350g, cleaned
   and sliced
350–400g **floury potatoes**, peeled
   and cut into chunks
2 teaspoons **sea salt**
1 litre **water**
125ml **double cream**
1 tablespoon chopped
   fresh flat-leaf parsley
freshly ground black pepper

1. Put the leek and potatoes into a heavy-based saucepan. Add the salt and the water and bring to the boil. Simmer until soft and cooked through, about 30–35 minutes. Then turn off the heat and, with a hand blender, whizz until smooth.

2. Add the cream and stir it into the soup, then add the parsley and a few grinds of black pepper. Taste and adjust the seasoning, and serve with crusty bread.

Roasted Pumpkin Soup with a Zing

SERVES 4 · PREPARATION TIME: 15 MINUTES · COOKING TIME: 15 MINUTES · ♥ WF GF V

Creamy and comforting, this brightly coloured soup will cheer up even the darkest autumn day. To jazz it up a bit, we've added ground cumin and coriander for warmth.

1 **pumpkin**, deseeded, cut into
  wedges: about 1.25kg in
  prepared weight
3–4 sprigs of **fresh thyme**
2 tablespoons **olive oil**
725ml good **vegetable**
  or **chicken stock**
1–2 teaspoons **ground cumin**
1–2 teaspoons **ground coriander**
2 **limes**, cut into wedges, to serve
2 teaspoons **dried chilli flakes**,
  to garnish
salt and **freshly ground black pepper**

1. Heat the oven to 180°C/350°F/gas mark 4.

2. Pop the pumpkin wedges and the thyme into a large roasting tray, coat with the olive oil and season with salt and pepper. Place in the oven for 45 minutes to an hour, or until it's really soft and tender. Note, it could take even longer – every pumpkin is individual – just keep checking on it until it's done.

3. When the pumpkin is cooked, set it aside to cool, then scrape the flesh away from the skin. If it comes away in whole slices, cut it into 2cm chunks. Then put it into a pan with the stock and blitz with an immersion blender until you have a creamy consistency.

4. Add the spices and heat through for about 5 minutes. Then taste and add seasoning.

5. Serve in bowls, with the lime wedges and little piles of chilli on the side.

Belinda's Chicken Noodle Soup

SERVES 4 • PREPARATION TIME: 10 MINUTES • COOKING TIME: 10 MINUTES • ♥ ✓WF GF DF

A quick and healthy week-night supper.

1 litre **chicken stock**
2 free-range **chicken breasts**
2 cloves of **garlic**
200g mixed **shiitake** and **chestnut mushrooms**
100g **pak choi**
a large handful of **fresh coriander**
2 tablespoons **peanut oil**
200g **rice noodles**
3 tablespoons **soy sauce**
2 tablespoons **toasted sesame oil**

1. Put the chicken stock into a saucepan, put a lid on and bring to the boil. Cut the chicken breasts into small chunks.

2. Peel and finely slice the garlic. Generously slice the mushrooms. Chop the pak choi and coriander roughly.

3. Pour the peanut oil into a hot wok or wide heavy-based pan. When it smokes, add the garlic just for seconds and immediately follow with the chicken and mushrooms. Keep tossing until cooked (about 5–7 minutes). Add the soy sauce and sesame oil and keep tossing until absorbed.

4. Add the rice noodles and pak choi to the hot chicken stock, put a lid on and boil for 3–4 minutes. Pour the contents of the wok into the pan of stock and noodles and sprinkle with the coriander. Eat at once.

Belinda, my stepmother, appears effortlessly to combine managing a large extended family, a doctorate and a new career in psychology with the production of enormous feasts whenever family and friends descend upon her house (which is quite often). This is one of her staple suppers.

HENRY

TIPS

* Depending on what brand of rice noodles you use, you may need to add extra stock – some soak up more juice than others.

* A squeeze of lime on top before you eat is a nice addition.

Bacon & Root Veg Soup

A winter warmer and a Mima staple.

100g **streaky bacon**
1 large **onion**
150g **carrots**
150g **swede**
150g **waxy potatoes**
350g **parsnips**
2 tablespoons **olive oil**
2 **bay leaves**
1.5 litres **chicken stock**
100g grated **Cheddar** or **Parmesan cheese**
sea salt and **freshly ground black pepper**

1. Cut the bacon into small pieces. Peel and chop the onion. Peel and dice the carrots, swede, potatoes and parsnips.

2. Heat the oil in a heavy-bottomed pan. Add the bacon and fry until it is just getting crispy. Add the onion, and cook until it is getting soft.

3. Add all the diced vegetables and the bay leaves, and cook over a gentle heat with the lid on for 10 minutes, stirring occasionally.

4. Add the stock and simmer for 15 minutes, or until the vegetables are tender.

5. Season to taste and serve in bowls, sprinkled with the cheese.

TIPS

* Vegetarians can use garlic instead of the bacon, and vegetable stock instead of chicken stock.

* You can use any surplus root vegetables you have lying about. Celeriac tastes great alongside or instead of parsnip.

SALADS

Bean Salad with Pickled Onions

SERVES 4 · PREPARATION TIME: 15 MINUTES · COOKING TIME: NONE · ♥ ✓ WF GF DF V

Simple, fresh and healthy – pickling the onions like this sweetens them and takes away the raw onion flavour.

1 clove of **garlic**
1 **lemon**
a large handful of chopped
   fresh flat-leaf parsley
1 large **red onion**
2 **vine-ripened tomatoes**
2 tablespoons **extra virgin olive oil**
2 x 400g tins of **cannellini beans**
sea salt and **freshly ground black pepper**

1. Peel the garlic. On the finest holes of your grater, grate the garlic and lemon zest and mix it in a small bowl with the chopped parsley.

2. Peel the red onion and slice as finely as you can. Put the slices into a bowl with a few pinches of sea salt and the lemon juice. Leave for 5 minutes.

3. Chop the tomatoes into rough chunks. Season with salt and add them to the onions, along with the olive oil and the drained beans. Toss really well to combine the flavours. Season.

4. Leave the salad to sit until you get a nice pooling of tomato juice at the bottom – the magic juice. This will take around 5–10 minutes.

5. When ready to eat, stir in the parsley, lemon and garlic mix, then serve.

TIPS

* Serve with sourdough toast for a simple supper.

* Add toasted seeds or almonds.

* Substitute other fresh green herbs for the parsley.

* There are three things that raise this dish above the ordinary: the pickled onions; letting it sit so the juices steep; and the raw parsley, lemon and garlic mix at the end. You can try all sorts of combinations of different beans and vegetables (raw, grated courgettes are a good addition, as is grated carrot).

Laura's Jewelled Salad

SERVES 4 • PREPARATION TIME: 5 MINUTES • COOKING TIME: 5 MINUTES • ♥ WF V

200g **barley couscous**
200g good-quality **feta cheese**
1 **cucumber**
a bunch of mixed **fresh green herbs**,
   e.g. mint and coriander
100g **pine nuts**
seeds of 1 large **pomegranate**
2 cloves of **garlic**
2 tablespoons **extra virgin olive oil**
juice of 1½ **lemons**
sea salt and **freshly ground black pepper**

1. Prepare the couscous as per the instructions on the packet. Leave to cool in a large bowl.

2. Crumble the feta and cut the cucumber into chunks. Add these to the bowl, then roughly tear the herbs and add them too.

3. Lightly toast the pine nuts in a frying pan over a low heat, and scatter these and the pomegranate seeds over the salad.

4. Peel and finely mince or grate the garlic. Whisk together the olive oil, lemon juice and garlic and pour over the salad. Season well with salt and pepper, and serve.

Thirtieth Birthday Pea Salad

SERVES 4 · PREPARATION TIME: 5 MINUTES · COOKING TIME: 10 MINUTES · ♥ ✓ WF GF DF V

1 **red pepper**
2.5cm piece of **fresh ginger**
2 cloves of **garlic**
6 **spring onions**
2 tablespoons **extra virgin olive oil**
1 teaspoon **black mustard seeds**
1 teaspoon **red wine vinegar**
250g **frozen peas**
a small handful of **fresh coriander**, washed
   and chopped
sea salt and **freshly ground black pepper**

1. Halve and deseed the pepper, and cut into slices. Peel and grate the ginger and garlic. Trim the spring onions and cut on the diagonal into long thin strips.

2. Heat the olive oil in a saucepan over a medium heat and fry the mustard seeds until they pop. Swirl in the garlic and ginger.

3. Add the pepper, stirring well until it picks up some colour. Add the spring onions and the vinegar. It will sizzle a bit.

4. Throw in the peas with a tiny splash of water and leave to defrost and warm up, stirring occasionally. You are not looking to cook them, just to get them up to room temperature.

5. Remove from the heat. Season and add the chopped coriander.

I first made this salad at my joint 30th birthday party with my friends Simon and Roly. We made it for about 150 people, dressing it by tossing it in (clean) black bin liners – a useful trick.

HENRY

Carrots & Beetroots WITH TOASTED ALMONDS

SERVES 4 • PREPARATION TIME: 5 MINUTES • COOKING TIME: 45 MINUTES • ♥ ✓ WF GF DF V

Beautiful to look at and extremely straightforward to make.

750g whole **raw beetroots**, peeled and cut into chunks
750g **carrots**, peeled and cut into batons
4 tablespoons **extra virgin olive oil**
1½ tablespoons **runny honey**
1 tablespoon **balsamic vinegar**
80g **flaked almonds**
3 tablespoons **fresh chervil** or **parsley leaves** (optional)
sea salt and **freshly ground black pepper**

1. Preheat the oven to 200°C/400°F/gas mark 6.

2. Put the beetroots and carrots into separate oven dishes, coat with olive oil and season well with salt and pepper. Add the honey to the carrots and the balsamic to the beetroot and stir well.

3. Put both trays into the oven for 45 minutes, or until the carrots are starting to brown and the beetroots are soft.

4. Meanwhile, dry-toast the almonds in a frying pan over a medium heat, being careful not to burn them. Chop the parsley, if using.

5. Place the vegetables on a serving dish. Scatter over the chervil or parsley and the almonds before serving.

Warm Anchovy, Garlic & Potato Salad

SERVES 4 • PREPARATION TIME: 5 MINUTES • COOKING TIME: 20 MINUTES • ♥ WF GF DF

Pouring a dressing on to warm potatoes has a wonderful effect, as the potatoes soften and absorb the flavours. This dish is very moreish.

800g **new potatoes**
3 cloves of **garlic**
2 tablespoons **white wine vinegar**
1 x 50g **tin of anchovy fillets**
100ml **extra virgin olive oil**
1 tablespoon **finely chopped fresh chives**
sea salt and **freshly ground black pepper**

1. Chop the potatoes in half and boil them, covered, in a large pan of salted water until tender.

2. Put the garlic, vinegar and anchovies into a blender and whizz to form a paste. With the blender running, drizzle in the extra virgin olive oil. Season.

3. Drain the potatoes and pour the dressing over them, tossing them well.

4. Allow to cool for 3 minutes, then toss again. Sprinkle with the chopped chives and serve.

TIPS

* It is a good idea to cut the potatoes in half with a fork once cooked, so that they are roughed up and absorb the anchovy dressing.

* You can use parsley in the place of chives.

* If you can't get hold of new potatoes, any waxy potatoes will do. If you use bigger ones, peel them and chop them into chunks.

* Great as a side salad at a barbecue. Make it in the morning and serve it later at room temperature.

3 Sisters Superfood Salad

SERVES 4 • PREPARATION TIME: 15–20 MINUTES • COOKING TIME: 35 MINUTES • ♥ ✓ DF V

These 3 sisters – corn, beans and squash – and their friends really pack a punch: a vibrant, delicious, colourful salad that showcases big, bold flavours influenced by the fusion of the new and old worlds.

300g **pumpkin**, peeled weight (approximately 350g before peeling), cut into 3–4cm cubes
4–6 small **purple potatoes**
a little **olive oil**
2 **cobs of corn**
4 large handfuls of **mixed leaves**
200g **sprouted beans** and **seeds**
4 **spring onions**, trimmed and sliced on the diagonal
1 **avocado**, cut into 2–3cm pieces

100g **pomegranate seeds**
a handful of **pumpkin seeds**
a good sprinkling of **gomasio** (available from health food stores)

For the dressing:
2 tablespoons **lemon juice**
½ tablespoon **tamari**
1 tablespoon **rice vinegar**
3 tablespoons **mild olive oil**

1. Bring 2 large pans of lightly salted water to the boil. Pop the pumpkin pieces into one and simmer until they are just tender – about 8–10 minutes. Stick a knife in to test for doneness – we want them tender but not collapsing. Drain, run under some cold water to stop them cooking, then set aside to cool.

2. In the other pan, add the whole purple potatoes and cook until just done, about 15–20 minutes depending on your spud size. Drain and set aside to cool.

3. Meanwhile, heat a griddle pan. Lightly oil the corn cobs and place them on the heated griddle. Keep turning them until they are cooked through and have some nice char-marks on the sides – about 10 minutes. Remove and set aside to cool.

4. To make the dressing, mix all the ingredients together well. Taste and adjust the seasoning if you like. We want a salty/sour/umami flavour.

5. Now take a sharp knife and, holding the corn vertically, gently slice off the kernels.

6. Divide the leaves evenly between 4 bowls and sprinkle over the sprouted seeds and beans.

7. Slice the potatoes into discs and add them, together with the pumpkin, spring onions, avocado and corn kernels, to the bowls. Scatter the pomegranate seeds over each portion.

8. Pour over the dressing and sprinkle over the pumpkin seeds and gomasio to serve.

TIPS

* This salad stands up well on its own, but you can also add grilled chicken or fish. If that's how you'd like to serve it, this recipe will serve 6.

Gill's Spinach, Chorizo & Halloumi Salad

SERVES 4 • PREPARATION TIME: 15 MINUTES • COOKING TIME: 20 MINUTES • ✓

Actually, this was created by Gill's friend Jane, but it comes to us via Gill, so we're putting her name on it. It's a salad that uses up the kinds of things you find in the fridge during the summer.

4 large handfuls of **baby spinach leaves,** washed
250g **halloumi cheese**, cut into 4 pieces
2 fat cloves of **garlic**, crushed
4 tablespoons **extra virgin olive oil**
24 spears of **fresh asparagus**, trimmed
150g **chorizo**, thinly sliced
4 tablespoons **balsamic syrup**
salt and **freshly ground black pepper**

1. Divide the spinach between 4 large plates.

2. Lay the halloumi flat in a bowl. Mix the crushed garlic and olive oil together and pour it over the pieces of cheese leaving them for a few minutes to marinate.

3. Put a grill pan over a medium to high heat until it's very hot. Put the asparagus into a bowl and toss it in a little olive oil until it's well coated. Season with a pinch of salt, then chargrill the asparagus spears until they are nice and lined or charred. You may want to cut a few in half lengthways before putting them on the grill if they are really fat. Divide the asparagus between the bowls.

4. Now fry the slices of halloumi, pouring the marinade into the pan with them. Cook the cheese until it starts to go golden on the outside. Divide it evenly between the salad bowls, laying it on top of the asparagus.

5. Finally, pan-fry the chorizo in a clean frying pan. As it cooks, it will release lots of its spicy oils. This is a good thing! When the sausage starts to get a little crispy on the outside, divide it up, along with the juices, on top of the salad bowls.

6. Drizzle over any more olive oil that you might think is needed, and finish off with a little salt, lots of pepper, and a tablespoon of balsamic syrup per serving.

Mackerel Skies Salad

SERVES 4 AS A MAIN COURSE, OR 6 AS A STARTER • PREPARATION TIME: 15 MINUTES
COOKING TIME: NONE • ♥ ✓ WF GF DF

This is FULL of omega-3 fatty acids and vitamin C, and packed with wonderful agrodolce flavour. It's quick to make, and it's colourful, too – just like a sunrise on a plate.

1 large **carrot**, grated into long strips

1 small **red pepper**, deseeded and sliced into strips

¼ of a small **white cabbage**, shredded

1 small **raw beetroot**, peeled and grated

½ a large **cucumber**, peeled and sliced into small cubes

200g **hot-smoked mackerel**, peeled and flaked

1 tablespoon **toasted flax seeds**

For the dressing:
3 tablespoons **olive oil**
the juice of ½ a large **orange**
3 teaspoons r**ed wine vinegar**
a good pinch of **sea salt**
freshly ground black pepper

1. Mix all the vegetables together in a large bowl. Mix the ingredients for the dressing together in clean jam jar, shake, and stir thoroughly into the vegetables.

2. Stir in the flaked smoked mackerel, or scatter it on the top. Up to you. Finish with the toasted flax seeds.

TIPS

* Instead of mackerel, you could use hot-smoked trout or salmon. Smoked chicken works, too.

* Sometimes Kay leaves out the fish and uses the salad as a base for leftover duck or turkey.

* Mix up the seeds – we love the crunch and flavour of toasted flax seeds, but pumpkin or sunflower would be great, too, as would walnut pieces.

A Few Words About Mackerel

Iridescent, shiny and as fast a bullet; as fish go, it's just about as healthy as it's possible to be. It's full of omega-3 fatty acids, vitamin B12 and selenium. At the time of writing, it's one of the most sustainable fish in the sea. (Let's hope it stays that way.) And it's delicious. Smoked, grilled, steamed or roasted – and even raw – it's packed with flavour. Here are a couple of easy suggestions for mackerel-based lunchtime salads.

Four Simple Dressings

Tapenade Dressing

MAKES 100ML · PREPARATION TIME: 3 MINUTES · COOKING TIME: NONE
♥ ✓ WF DF GF (V IF YOU USE ANCHOVY-FREE TAPENADE)

Best used to dress strong-flavoured salad leaves or cooked greens.

2 tablespoons **tapenade**
1 tablespoon **sherry vinegar**
5 tablespoons **extra virgin olive oil**
sea salt and **freshly ground black pepper**

1. Put all the ingredients into a jam jar.

2. Shake well, and check the seasoning.

Leon House Dressing

MAKES 450ML · PREPARATION TIME: 3 MINUTES · COOKING TIME: NONE · ♥ ✓ WF DF GF V

Gives a real punch to old fashioned lettuce leaves. Keeps well in the fridge.

2 tablespoons **Dijon mustard**
80ml **white wine vinegar**
350ml **rapeseed oil**
sea salt and **freshly ground black pepper**

1. Blend the mustard and vinegar in a blender.

2. Keeping the blender running, slowly add the rapeseed oil until you have a fully emulsified dressing.

3. Season carefully.

Balsamic Dressing

MAKES 75ML • PREPARATION TIME: 3 MINUTES • COOKING TIME: NONE • ♥ ✓ WF DF GF V

Best for simple green salads with lots of chopped herbs in them.

2 tablespoons **balsamic vinegar**
(use a nice syrupy aged one if you can)
6 tablespoons **extra virgin olive oil**
(a good one really makes a difference)
sea salt and **freshly ground black pepper**

1. Put the ingredients straight on to the salad.

2. Grind over lots of black pepper and add a generous amount of salt.

3. Toss with vigour.

Oriental Dressing

MAKES 75ML • PREPARATION TIME: 8 MINUTES • COOKING TIME: NONE • ♥ ✓ WF DF GF V

Best on shredded vegetables – for example, grated carrot and courgette or finely shredded Chinese cabbage.

1 fat clove of **garlic**
1cm piece of **fresh ginger**
1 **spring onion**
½ a **fresh red chilli**
1 tablespoon **fish sauce**
juice of ½ a **lime**
3 tablespoons **peanut oil** or other flavourless oil
1 tablespoon **toasted sesame oil**

TIPS

* You can add a little honey if you like your dressing sweet.

1. In a small clean jar with a lid, use your finest grater to grate the garlic and ginger into the jar.

2. Finely slice the spring onion and deseed and finely chop the chilli. Add to the jar.

3. Measure in the fish sauce and lime juice and add the oils. Screw on the lid and shake well.

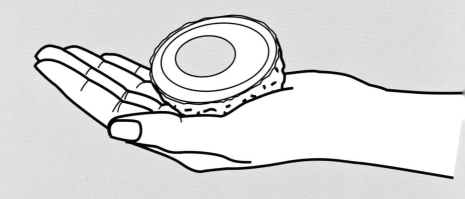

SNACKS

Benny's Scotch Eggs

SERVES 6 · PREPARATION TIME: 30 MINUTES PLUS COOLING · COOKING TIME: 20 MINUTES · ♥ ✓ WF GF

Benny Peverelli was a key part of the Leon team for eight years, a lot of that time as Executive Head Chef or Chief Foodie Personage. We love him. And we love his Scotch eggs.

7 **free-range eggs**,
    at room temperature
4–5 **rice cakes**
rapeseed oil, for deep frying (we
    reckon you'll need about a litre)

125g **rice flour**
2 tablespoons **milk**
6 **wheat-free, gluten-free pork
    sausages**

1. Ensure your eggs are at room temperature, then bring a medium pan of water to the boil. Gently lower 6 of the eggs into the boiling water and cook them for 6 minutes for soft centres, or 9 minutes for hard yolks.

2. Once the eggs are cooked, run them under cold water for 10 minutes to cool them down.

3. Gently tap the eggs all over to crack the shell, then peel them carefully as they will be soft. (Every time you take a bit of peel off, you should dip your fingers back into the water otherwise they may become tacky and you could break the egg.)

4. To make the crumb, break the rice cakes into small pieces, then pop them into a food processor and whizz for a minute or so.

5. Heat the rapeseed oil to 180°C in a deep-fat fryer. (You can do this in a heavy-based saucepan over a medium heat, but be very VERY careful. You do so at your own risk.)

6. While the oil is heating, prepare your crumbing station: take 3 bowls and place your flour in one, your crumbed rice cakes in another, then break your final egg into the third bowl and whisk in the milk.

7. Cut out 2 large squares of clingfilm. Place one on your work surface and leave the other for later.

8. Now take a sharp knife and run it down the length of one of the sausages. Squeeze the contents of the sausage into your hand and squash together to form a ball. Repeat with the remaining sausages.

Then place each sausage ball on the clingfilm. Put the other piece of clingfilm over the top and squash down until you have 6 sausage ovals, about 0.5cm thick.

9. Next dry your boiled eggs with a little kitchen paper and place one into the flour, coating it all over (this will help the sausagemeat stick). Peel a sausagemeat disc off the clingfilm and lay it over the egg. Gently fold the sausagemeat around the egg and press the join together. Put to one side. Repeat with the other eggs.

10. Now take a small bowl of water and dampen your hands. Use your damp hands to smooth the sausage-coated eggs and turn them into smooth egg shapes.

11. Take an egg shape and gently roll it all over in the flour. Then place it in the egg and milk mixture and coat fully. Now place it in the rice cakes crumbs and cover all over, patting the egg to make sure it all sticks. Repeat this for each egg.

12. Check your oil is hot enough by dropping a small piece of bread into the oil – if it gently bubbles and fries, it's the right temperature. Using a slotted spoon, gently lower your egg into the oil, making sure you keep splashing oil over it if it's not fully covered. Fry for 10 minutes (or 5 on each side if your egg is not fully covered), cooking up to 3 eggs at a time.

13. Once they're cooked, place the eggs on kitchen paper to drain. Leave for 10 minutes to cool, then tuck in with some brown sauce.

Ana's Cheese Empanadas

MAKES 20 SMALL EMPANADAS · PREPARATION TIME: 30 MINUTES + 30 MINUTES RESTING TIME · COOKING TIME: 10–15 MINUTES · V

Our Ecuadorian cleaner Ana doesn't speak much English, but makes herself understood through the language of laughter, kindness and exceptionally good empanadas. Great party food.

400g **plain flour**
2 teaspoons **baking powder**
1 teaspoon **salt**
115g **butter**
50ml **orange juice**
80ml **sparkling water**
250g **mozzarella cheese**
1 **onion** grated or finely chopped
1½–2 tablespoons **caster sugar**,
    plus extra for sprinkling on top
    (optional)
1 **free-range egg**, lightly beaten
vegetable oil, for frying (optional)

1. Put the flour, baking powder and salt into a food processor and whizz until well mixed.

2. Add the butter, orange juice and sparkling water and process until a dough forms.

3. Tip the dough on to a surface, bring it together into a ball, wrap it in clingfilm and place in the fridge for 30 minutes to rest.

4. Grate the mozzarella into a bowl and add the onion. Add the sugar and mix well.

5. Preheat the oven to 200°C/400°F/gas mark 6. Line a baking sheet with baking paper, or oil it well.

6. When the dough has rested remove it from the clingfilm and dust your work surface with flour. Cut the ball of dough in half (it's easier to roll out smaller amounts). Roll out the dough so that it's only a couple of millimetres thick.

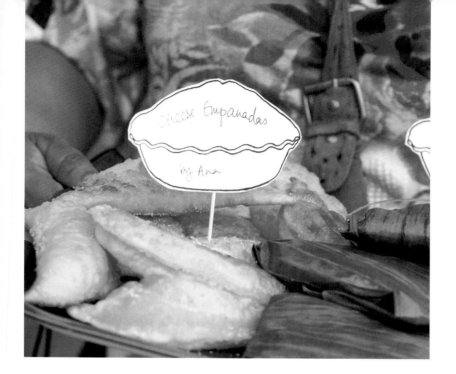

7. Using a 9–10cm cutter, cut circles out of the dough. Place a teaspoon of the cheese filling in the centre of each circle, fold the dough over to make a half-moon shape, and seal the discs pressing down with a fork. Make sure they are all well sealed, otherwise the filling will ooze out when you cook them.

8. Brush the empanadas with the beaten egg, and sprinkle a little sugar over the top of each one if you want that extra sweetness. Place on the baking tray and cook in the oven for 10–15 minutes, until golden. Cool on a wire rack.

9. If you fancy the fried option, fill a saucepan 3–4cm deep with vegetable oil. When the oil is hot, deep-fry the empanadas until golden, and sprinkle with caster sugar before serving.

Things on Spuds

SERVES 4 • PREPARATION TIME: 5 MINUTES • COOKING TIME: I HOUR • ♥ ✓ WF GF DF V

Sometimes there's nothing better than a hot baked potato, crusty on the outside and steaming and soft within, just begging to be buttered. But what else can we do with them? Here are some suggestions from family and friends to making the best baked spuds ever…

1. Pick your potato – this is very important. Buy a variety that bakes well – floury types are best. We recommend King Edwards.

2. Heat the oven to 220°C/425°F/gas mark 7.

3. Wash the spuds under cold, running water. Shake them a little to remove the excess water, but don't dry them completely.

4. Roll them in some sea salt.

5. Pop them straight into the oven, directly on to the shelf. Bake them for about an hour – it depends on the size of your potato. Just poke them with a skewer to test for 'give' and doneness.

6. Take them out and let everyone admire their crispy exterior and wow at their fluffy insides.

Some ideas for toppings, from left to right:

Georgia's Eggy Potato

Scoop out the insides of the cooked potato. Mash it in a bowl with a lightly beaten egg, then season with salt and pepper. Add some crisply fried bacon bits (or leftover ham), and some cheese if you like… or any bits of cooked veggies you have to hand. Scoop it all back into the potato skin, top with a little butter, and pop back in the oven for 15 minutes, or until it's puffy and crispy on top.

Cheesy Spinach & Mushrooms

This is for Abi and Issy, the vegetarian element of our team. Sauté some sliced mushrooms in a little olive oil and butter with a sprinkle of garlic and parsley, and set aside. Then wilt down a handful or two of spinach in the same pan. Season with salt and pepper. Pile it on to the potato with the mushrooms and top with some cubes of Gruyère cheese.

Eleanor's Top Table

Eleanor is John's younger daughter. One day at school in year 1 she was allowed to sit on Top Table with Mr and Mrs Heinrich, and to have baked potatoes with her favourite topping: lashings of butter and EXTRA grated Cheddar cheese, salt and pepper. Now that's what we call TOP marks.

Beetroot, Crème Fraîche & Chives

Simply chop some cooked (not pickled) beetroot into cubes. Spoon a splodge of crème fraîche on to the buttered potato. Scatter over the beetroot and finish with chopped fresh chives, salt and pepper.

Herb Butter

Very retro, but very good. Make the herb butter of your choice – we use finely chopped fresh parsley, garlic, fresh thyme and salt and pepper mashed into some softened unsalted butter. If you have time, using some clingfilm or foil, roll the soft butter into a sausage shape and refrigerate it. Then just slice off a few discs and place them artfully in a steaming, split potato.

The Leftover Spud

Baked potatoes take to leftovers like ducks to water (actually, leftover duck would be fantastic). So use 'em up.

THE LEFTOVER SPUD

Arthur's Favourite Duck & Lettuce Wraps

SERVES 4 CHILDREN · PREPARATION TIME: 5 MINUTES · COOKING TIME: 25 MINUTES · WF GF DF

A healthy and fun dish for the children to help make.

> 1 **cucumber**
> 2 **little gem lettuces**
> 1 **duck breast**
> **olive oil**
> a jar of **plum sauce**
> **sea salt** and **freshly ground black pepper**

1. Preheat the oven to 190°C/375°F/gas mark 5. Cut the cucumber into batons and put into a bowl. Separate the lettuce leaves and put into a second bowl.

2. Season the duck breast and add a dash of olive oil and roast for about 25 minutes, until the skin is crispy. Separate the cooked meat into little bits, using 2 forks.

3. Get the children to make parcels, wrapping the duck and cucumber in the lettuce leaves, and serve the plum sauce separately on the side in a small bowl.

Fish Finger Wrap

SERVES 2 • PREPARATION TIME: 10 MINUTES • COOKING TIME: 20 MINUTES • ♥ ✓

Every kid's favourite… in a wrap.

4 **fish fingers**
2 good-quality **flatbreads**
2 tablespoons good **tartare sauce**
4–6 **gherkins**, sliced
Cos lettuce leaves, shredded

a pinch of chopped **fresh dill**
a squeeze of **lemon juice**
salt and **freshly ground black pepper**

1. Cook the fish fingers and heat up your flatbreads as per the packet instructions.

2. Spread some tartare sauce on to the warmed flatbreads, and top with a few slices of gherkin. Add some lettuce, then the crisply cooked fish fingers. Add a little sprinkling of freshly chopped dill, season with salt and pepper, and get fancy with a squeeze of fresh lemon juice to finish. Wrap and eat.

Leon's Halloumi Wrap

SERVES 2 • PREPARATION TIME: 10 MINUTES • COOKING TIME: 6 MINUTES • ♥ ✓ V

This is based on the popular wrap we had on the menu for a while. Time to bring it back?

2 tablespoons good **mango chutney**
2 gluten-free **flatbreads**, or the flatbread of your choice
200g **halloumi cheese**, sliced and marinated in **olive oil**, crushed **garlic** and **thyme leaves**

2 **carrots**, peeled and grated
2 tablespoons **fresh flat-leaf parsley**, chopped
salt and **freshly ground black pepper**

1. Spread the mango chutney thinly on the flatbread of your choice.

2. Drain the halloumi and grill it for 3 minutes or so on each side, until golden brown.

3. Pop half the halloumi into each flatbread (heat them up if you like) and add the carrot, parsley and freshly ground pepper. And some salt if you really want it. Wrap and eat.

Things on Toast

SERVES 4 • PREPARATION TIME: 15 MINUTES • COOKING TIME: 10 MINUTES • ♥ ✓ WF GF DF V

Toast, glorious toast. Sometimes we just need to jazz it up a bit. Here are some suggestions from the Leon team:

Brown Crab, Lemon & Dill

Spread some thick brown crabmeat on your toast. Squeeze over some lemon juice. Finish with freshly ground black pepper and a scattering of chopped fresh dill.

Marmite, Avocado, Tomato, Basil & Gomasio

Kay's favourite: spread a smear of good unsalted butter on the toast. Then a smear of Marmite. Follow this with sliced avocados and halved cherry tomatoes. Scatter a few fresh basil leaves on top and finish with a good grinding of black pepper and a sprinkle of Gomasio.

Graig Farm's All Meat Sausage on Fig Jam

Grill or oven-roast some sausages until cooked. Spread the toast with a thick layer of fig jam. Slice the sausages in half lengthways and lay them on the toast.

Poached Egg & Sautéd Mushrooms

Slice some mushrooms and sauté them with some garlic in a little olive oil. Sprinkle in a few leaves of fresh thyme or some chopped fresh parsley. Set aside to keep warm. Meanwhile, poach an egg, then pile the mushrooms on the toast with the poached egg on top.

Goat's Cheese, Honey, Thyme & Walnuts

Cut a goat's cheese log (the type with rind) into slices. Place 2 or 3 slices overlapping on each slice of toast. Pop under a hot grill for 1 minute or so, just to get the cheese slightly melt-y. Drizzle with honey and scatter with chopped walnuts and fresh thyme.

Cinnamon Butter with Sliced Apples

Mix some softened butter with a good pinch of ground cinnamon and a squeeze of agave nectar. Spread on the toast. Place slices of raw apple on top. Sprinkle with a final dusting of cinnamon.

Dips

Hummus

SERVES 4–6 • PREPARATION TIME: 10 MINUTES • COOKING TIME: NONE • ♥ ✓ WF GF V

Everybody loves hummus. Our supermarkets sell it by the tonne – literally. But have you seen what's written on the label? Try this homemade version, and cut out the additives.

1 x 400g tin of **chickpeas**, drained
1–2 cloves of **garlic**, peeled
2 tablespoons **tahini**
2 tablespoons **olive oil**
6 tablespoons **water**

the juice of ½ a **lemon**
a large pinch of **salt**
a drizzle of **extra virgin olive oil**
a sprinkle of **ground sumac** and/
or **ground cumin** (optional)

1. Just place everything except the extra virgin olive oil and the sumac/cumin in a food processor and whizz until smooth. Taste and adjust the seasoning.

2. Serve in a bowl, drizzled with a little extra virgin olive oil. Sprinkle with the sumac and/or cumin if you like.

Lentil Masala Dip

ERVES 4–6 • PREPARATION TIME: 5 MINUTES + COOLING • COOKING TIME: 10–20 MINUTES • ♥ ✓ WF GF V

Fragrant with curry and very more-ish.

140g **red lentils**
1 teaspoon **Madras curry powder**
a pinch of **ground ginger**

a small handful of **fresh coriander**, chopped
salt and **freshly ground black pepper**

1. Rinse the lentils well under running water – you want to get rid of any grit or sand. Put them into a saucepan and cover them with fresh cold water.

2. Bring to the boil and simmer for about 15 minutes, or according to the packet instructions. Drain and set aside to cool.

3. Once the lentils have cooled, whizz them in a food processor with the curry powder, ground ginger, salt and pepper. Taste and adjust the seasoning, then stir in the chopped coriander and serve.

Tangy Cheese Dip (Cheez Whiz)

SERVES 4 • PREPARATION TIME: 10 MINUTES • COOKING TIME: NONE • ♥ ✓ WF GF V

Cottage cheese isn't just for diet fruit plates.

400g **cottage cheese**
1 clove of **garlic**, peeled and chopped
1 tablespoon **Worcestershire sauce**
1 teaspoon **tomato ketchup**
½ teaspoon **Tabasco sauce**
a good squeeze of **lime** or **lemon juice**
1 tablespoon chopped **fresh chives**
4 **cherry tomatoes**, deseeded and chopped
a small handful of **fresh coriander**, chopped
1 large **red chilli**, deseeded and slivered (optional)
salt and **freshly ground black pepper**

1. Whizz everything except the chives, tomatoes, coriander and chilli in a food processor. Taste and adjust the seasoning. You want a little spice, some sharpness and some sweetness.

2. Pour into a serving bowl and gently stir in the chives and tomatoes. Scatter some chopped coriander and the slivered chillies on top.

Kay's Guacamole

SERVES 4 • PREPARATION TIME: 10 MINUTES • COOKING TIME: NONE • ♥ ✓ WF GF DF V

Rich, green and good for you.

1 clove of **garlic**, peeled
2 ripe **avocados**, peeled and flesh scooped out
the juice of ½ a **lime**
2 **spring onions**, trimmed and finely chopped
a small handful of **fresh coriander**, finely chopped

½–1 **green serrano** or **jalapeño chilli**, deseeded and finely chopped (optional)
4 **cherry tomatoes**, sliced (optional)
sea salt, to taste

1. Using a big pestle and mortar or a molcajete, grind the garlic to a paste. Add the avocado and pound until mashed. Add the lime juice.

2. Stir in the chopped spring onions and the chopped coriander. If using, stir in the chillies and the tomatoes. Season to taste with salt.

Roasted Carrot & Cumin Dip

SERVES 4–6 • PREPARATION TIME: 10 MINUTES • COOKING TIME: 50 MINUTES • ♥ WF GF DF V

Healthy and simple. And bright orange.

700g **carrots**, roughly chopped
3 tablespoons **olive oil**
a pinch of **cane sugar** (optional)
1 teaspoon **ground cumin**
1 clove of **garlic**, peeled and roughly crushed
2 tablespoons **water**
salt and **freshly ground black pepper**

1. Heat the oven to 200°C/400°F/gas mark 6.

2. Tumble the carrots in a roasting tray with 1 tablespoon of the olive oil, a pinch of sugar (if you feel like it) and a good sprinkle of salt and pepper.

3. Cover with foil and roast for 45–50 minutes, or until a knife goes through the carrots easily.

4. Remove from the oven and cool slightly.

5. Once the carrots have cooled, put them into the food processor or blender and whizz, adding the cumin, garlic and the remaining 2 tablespoons of olive oil and the water, until you have a nice creamy consistency. Serve at room temperature.

CONVERSION CHART FOR COMMON MEASURES

LIQUIDS

15 ml	$^1/_2$ fl oz
25 ml	1 fl oz
50 ml	2 fl oz
75 ml	3 fl oz
100ml	3 $^1/_2$ fl oz
125 ml	4 fl oz
150 ml	$^1/_4$ pint
175 ml	6 fl oz
200 ml	7 fl oz
250 ml	8 fl oz
275 ml	9 fl oz
300 ml	$^1/_2$ pint
325 ml	11 fl oz
350 ml	12 fl oz
375 ml	13 fl oz
400 ml	14 fl oz
450 ml	$^3/_4$ pint
475 ml	16 fl oz
500 ml	17 fl oz
575 ml	18 fl oz
600 ml	1 pint
750 ml	1 $^1/_4$ pints
900 ml	1 $^1/_2$ pints
1 litre	1 $^3/_4$ pints
1.2 litres	2 pints
1.5 litres	2 $^1/_2$ pints
1.8 litres	3 pints
2 litres	3 $^1/_2$ pints
2.5 litres	4 pints
3.6 litres	6 pints

WEIGHTS

5 g	$^1/_4$ oz
15 g	$^1/_2$ oz
20 g	$^3/_4$ oz
25 g	1 oz
50 g	2 oz
75 g	3 oz
125 g	4 oz
150 g	5 oz
175 g	6 oz
200 g	7 oz
250 g	8 oz
275 g	9 oz
300 g	10 oz
325 g	11 oz
375 g	12 oz
400 g	13 oz
425 g	14 oz
475 g	15 oz
500 g	1 lb
625 g	1 $^1/_4$ lb
750 g	1 $^1/_2$ lb
875 g	1 $^3/_4$ lb
1 kg	2 lb
1.25 kg	2 $^1/_2$ lb
1.5 kg	3 lb
1.75 kg	3 $^1/_2$ lb
2 kg	4 lb

OVEN TEMPERATURES

110°C......(225°F).......Gas Mark $1/4$
120°C......(250°F).......Gas Mark $1/2$
140°C......(275°F).......Gas Mark 1
150°C......(300°F).......Gas Mark 2
160°C......(325°F).......Gas Mark 3
180°C......(350°F).......Gas Mark 4
190°C......(375°F).......Gas Mark 5
200°C......(400°F).......Gas Mark 6
220°C......(425°F).......Gas Mark 7
230°C......(450°F).......Gas Mark 8

MEASUREMENTS

5 mm .... $1/4$ inch
1 cm .... $1/2$ inch
1.5 cm .... $3/4$ inch
2.5 cm .... 1 inch
5 cm .... 2 inches
7 cm .... 3 inches
10 cm .... 4 inches
12 cm .... 5 inches
15 cm .... 6 inches
18 cm .... 7 inches
20 cm .... 8 inches
23 cm .... 9 inches
25 cm .... 10 inches
28 cm .... 11 inches
30 cm .... 12 inches
33 cm .... 13 inches

Working with different types of oven

All the recipes in this book have been tested in an oven without a fan. If you are using a fan-assisted oven, lower the temperature given in the recipe by 20°C. Modern fan-assisted ovens are very efficient at circulating heat evenly around the oven, so there's also no need to worry about positioning.

Regardless of what type of oven you use you will find that it has its idiosyncrasies, so don't stick slavishly to any baking recipes. Make sure you understand how your oven behaves and adjust accordingly.

Key to Symbols/Nutritional Info

♥   LOW SATURATED FATS
✓   LOW GLYCEMIC (GI) LOAD
WF   WHEAT FREE
GF   GLUTEN FREE
DF   DAIRY FREE
V   VEGETARIAN
🍴   INDULGENCE

🐦   COOKING TIPS, EXTRA INFORMATION
TIPS   AND ALTERNATIVE IDEAS.

Index

First published in Great Britain in 2013 by Conran Octopus Limited,
a part of Octopus Publishing Group,
Endeavour House, 189 Shaftesbury Avenue, London WC2H 8JY
www.octopusbooks.co.uk

An Hachette UK Company
www.hachette.co.uk

This book includes a selection of previously published recipes taken from the following titles:
Leon Naturally Fast Food; Leon Baking & Puddings; Leon Family & Friends.

British Library Cataloguing-in-Publication Data.
A catalogue record for this book is available from the British Library.

Publisher: Alison Starling
Senior Editor: Sybella Stephens
Assistant Editor: Stephanie Milner
Art Director: Jonathan Christie
Art Direction, Design and Illustrations: Anita Mangan
Design Assistant: Abigail Read
Photography: Georgia Glynn Smith
Production Manager: Katherine Hockley

ISBN 978 1 84091 622 5

Printed in China

A note from the authors…
Medium eggs should be used unless otherwise stated.
We have endeavoured to be as accurate as possible in all the preparation and cooking times listing
in the recipes in this book. However they are an estimate based on our own timings during recipe
testing, and should be taken as a guide only, not as the literal truth. We have also tried to source all
our food facts carefully, but we are not scientists. So our food facts and nutrition advice are not
absolute. If you feel you require consultation with a nutritionist, consult your GP for a recommendation.